# The Gospel of Universalism

## Hope, Courage, and the Love of God

Tom Owen-Towle

Boston: Skinner House Books

Copyright ©1993 by the Unitarian Universalist Association. All rights reserved. Published by Skinner House Books, an imprint of the Unitarian Universalist Association, 25 Beacon Street, Boston, MA 02108-2800.

Project Editor: Brenda Wong
Designer: Suzanne Morgan

ISBN 1-55896-315-4
Printed in the USA.

99 98 97 96
10 9 8 7 6 5 4 3 2

**Acknowledgments**
The lines from "Of Grief" and "A Hard Death" are reprinted from *Selected Poems of May Sarton,* edited by Serena Sue Hilsinger and Lois Brynes, by permission of W.W. Norton & Company, Inc. Copyright ©1978 by May Sarton.

          **Library of Congress Cataloging-in-Publication Data**
Owen-Towle, Tom.
    The Gospel of Universalism : hope, courage, and the love of God / Tom Owen Towle
        p.    cm.
    Includes bibliographical references.
    ISBN 1-55896-315-4
    1. Universalism. 2. Universalist churches—Apologetic works. 3. Unitarian Universalist churches—Apologetic works. 4. Universalists—United States.   I. Title.
BX9941.2.O94 1993
289.1'34—dc20
                                                       93-8307
                                                         CIP

# Table of Contents

| | |
|---|---|
| Introduction | v |

## Hope

| | |
|---|---|
| No-Hellites | 2 |
| Sailing the Straits | 4 |
| Let All Sorrows Ripen in Me | 7 |
| The Stuff of Eternity | 10 |
| The Larger Hope | 13 |
| Hopedale and Salubria | 15 |
| Happiness and Holiness Are Inseparable | 18 |
| Grand Possibilities Are All Before Us | 21 |
| Universalism Lives On | 24 |

## Courage

| | |
|---|---|
| Benevolence | 28 |
| Let Love Continue | 32 |
| Agitators For Equality | 35 |
| Patriots, One and All | 39 |
| Circuit Riders | 42 |
| Reluctant Reformers For Racial Justice | 45 |
| Lovers Tossed By These Difficult Times | 49 |
| Quintessential Bridger | 52 |
| Universalism Lives On | 54 |

## The Love of God

| | |
|---|---|
| Everlasting Love of God | 58 |
| Universalism Lives On | 61 |
| | |
| Notes | 64 |
| Selected Resources | 68 |
| Index of Universalist Contributors | 70 |

## Dedication

*The Gospel of Universalism* is dedicated to Harmon Gehr, Universalist minister and enduring friend, who, twenty-five years ago, graciously opened to me the hopeful, courageous, loving heritage of Universalism . . . just as I was emerging from the caverns of Calvinism and searching for a more spacious, inclusive religious home.

# Introduction

No more evocative summary of the Universalist path can be found than that uttered by John Murray (1741-1815):

> Go out into the highways and by-ways of America, your new country. Give the people, blanketed with a decaying and crumbling Calvinism, something of your new vision. You may possess only a small light but uncover it, let it shine, use it in order to bring more light and understanding to the hearts and minds of men and women. Give them, not Hell, but hope and courage. Do not push them deeper into their theological despair, but preach the kindness and everlasting love of God.

Nestled amid the theological timber of that familiar preachment lies a trio of foundational Universalist principles. Because John Murray was a trinitarian Universalist, he wouldn't flinch when I select hope, courage, and the love of God as the unifying themes for this book.

A sense of indomitable confidence, in both divinity and humanity, has been central to Universalism since its inception. Murray contended through word and deed that hope was inextricably linked to human courage and God's kindness. This book of essays illustrates the interrelatedness of these three bedrock Universalist values.

John Murray practiced what he preached. After suffering immense misfortune and tragedy in his homeland, including imprisonment for debts and the deaths of both his wife and infant child, Murray sailed from England to America, a despairing soul, set on "quitting the world."

Retirement, however, was not to be. After landing on

the New Jersey Coast, a providential wind from the heavens, combined with the unyielding enthusiasm of one Thomas Potter, waylaid Murray's early departure and returned the preacher to a pulpit. Settled once again in ministerial harness in the New World, Murray's courage was severely tested. Twentieth-century Universalist chronicler, Clinton Lee Scott, recounts:

> The heresy hunters were not long in finding their prey. Ministers in pulpit and in print assailed Murray, both his theology and his character. They succeeded in stirring up sentiment against him until he was looked upon by many as a public enemy. He was accused of being a British spy, and pelted with stones on the streets of Gloucester. The Gloucester Committee of Safety ordered Murray to leave town, but he refused to budge.

A dramatic incident ensued when a stone crashed through Murray's church window, narrowly missing his head. The dauntless preacher lifted the rock high and exclaimed, "This argument is solid and weighty, but it is neither reasonable nor convincing . . . not all the stones in Boston, except they stop my breath, shall shut my mouth."

Clearly, John Murray spoke from anguishing personal experience when he proclaimed, "Give them, not Hell, but hope and courage. . . ." He exemplified bravery.

In his final hour, Murray focused on God's boundless affection, the cornerstone virtue of his Universalist trinity. He sighed his last breath with this comforting reminder to his family, "Remember, there is One who loveth you, with an everlasting love, and who will never leave you nor forsake you."

In celebrating the abundant inspiration of American Universalism from 1793 until 1993, I have chosen stories and statements of Universalist exemplars—dead and living, familiar and unsung, laity and clergy, pietists and activists, theologians and educators—representing the various corners of our vast North American continent.

These women and men comprise different backgrounds and philosophies, but they have all been practicing Universalists who share a commitment to Murray's three essential principles. The lives of these Universalist companions have been grounded in hope, activated by courage, and sustained by God's love.

The primary purpose of *The Gospel of Universalism* is to activate our reflection and service as Unitarian Universalist heirs. While saluting the contributions of our Universalist sisters and brothers over the past two centuries, this volume is primarily neither a theological treatise nor a historical record. Those domains have been resourcefully addressed (note selected resources) by Universalist scholars and writers, in whose debt I stand and from whose wisdom I have generously drawn.

A word about 1793 as a significant anniversary date for American Universalism: 1793, the year when a yellow fever plague riddled the Philadelphia region; 1793, the year when Thomas Paine was imprisoned for writing his trenchant work, *The Age of Reason*; 1793, the year when Universalist medical missionary George de Benneville died. Seventeen nintey-three also marks the year when a relatively unrecognized event in American Universalist history transpired—the launching of the Universalist General Convention. Elmo Arnold Robinson recalls that momentous occasion:

> At that early Massachusetts center of Universalism, Oxford, there gathered on September 4th, 1793, "the Ministers, Elders, and Messengers, appointed by the Universal Churches and Societies in Massachusetts, Rhode Island, New Hampshire, Vermont, Connecticut, and New York." Unknowingly, without formal action, without constitution or by-laws, without officers or

funds, they laid the foundation of the Universalist General Convention, an organization which continued to function until its merger with the American Unitarian Association in 1961.

For our bicentennial Universalist celebrations, we have understandably turned to 1770 (when Murray's first sermon was delivered on American soil at Good Luck Point in New Jersey) or to 1780 (when the first Universalist church building was dedicated in Gloucester, Massachusetts) or to 1790 (when the initial Universalist statement, or declaration of faith, was adopted in Philadelphia). But 1793 documents the establishment of Universalism as an American denomination. It is an important benchmark, especially for a loosely confederated tribe of rugged individualists such as the Universalists.

So, two hundred years later, we gather, with an abundant mix of pride and gratitude, to pay homage to an unspectacular organizational moment that stands alongside previous celebrations of a Universalist sermon, building, and statement. Seventeen ninety-three honors an underrated event with enduring reverberations.

In 1793 Universalism brought good news to the American public through its life-enhancing theology: affirming the essential worth and dignity of every creature, affirming the illimitable love of God, affirming human redeemability, affirming virtue as its own reward, and affirming the universality of truths discoverable in all lands and eras. These Universalist principles are as relevant today as they were in 1793.

In a period of intransigent provincialism, our world hungers for a faith of inclusion. In a time when bigotry is rife and divine retribution is still promulgated from pulpits, contemporary civilization needs a hopeful, courageous religion of earthly compassion and heavenly acceptance.

Universalism, the largest word in any language and the broadest religious vision ever institutionalized in American history, has unequivocally asserted from its beginnings that a forged human-and-divine partnership is formidable enough to vanquish our living hells.

Universalism, from John Murray forward, has inspired humanity to exude hope, be brave, and rest assured that life is graciously embraced by the "One who loveth you, with an everlasting love. . . ."

# Hope

# No-Hellites

*If one believes that God is love and is incapable of condemning and destroying the innocent, one will have trouble with hell and infant damnation as the Universalists did.*
—Angus MacLean

The Universalists were known derisively in denominational circles as the "no-hellites." Whereas mainline American religion espoused the Calvinist doctrine of predestination (salvation for some, damnation for others), Universalists steadfastly believed that no God worth cherishing would ever condemn to eternal blaze the same creatures that deity lovingly infused with life.

Universalists, much to the chagrin of the orthodox, would even spin playful yarns, poking fun at the concept of a fiery pit. Our spiritual forebears took their religion seriously but never grimly. They employed humor as a healing balm in an often dreary, treacherous world. Once, when Hosea Ballou's doctrine of universal salvation was roundly questioned by his congregants who asked what he would do with persons who died reeking in sin and crime, Hosea replied, "I think it would be a good plan to bury them, don't you?" As Unitarian Universalist minister Charlotte Justice Saleska smilingly jests, "There was definitely no below for Mr. Ballou."

The no-hellites became an attractive, burgeoning religious alternative on the American scene, reportedly reaching status in 1888 as the sixth largest denomination in the United States. This hopeful faith helped to dampen the fires of hell in this land.

Nonetheless, the embers still smolder in contemporary society. A Princeton Religion Research Center survey recently asked, "Do you think there is a Hell, to which people who have led bad lives without being sorry are eternally damned?" and 53 percent of the respondents said yes. Unquestionably, the imagery of hell-fire and damnation still haunts people. Children lie awake at night sometimes in fear of the final judgment. Adults suffer torments of anxiety on their death beds. The doctrine of hell, however modernized, stands as official Christian dogma.

Universalists, while an undeniably cheerful lot, were hardly blind idealists. The no-hellites were no strangers to earthly hells of every variety, some of human creation and others beyond their control. They knew sin intimately but felt that honest self-appraisal and repentance would produce sufficient correction. There was no need for additional, let alone prolonged, punishment beyond the grave.

Furthermore, Universalists claimed sin to be a personal matter, eschewing the doctrine that we were paying for Adam's sin. Being unique individuals, we had ample opportunities during the earthly sojourn to do our own sinning, in short, to become original sinners.

As the twentieth century winds to a close, there is pressing need for a faith that aspires to diminish, if not quench, the fires of hell during this existence and beyond, whether on the streets or within the spirit.

Hallelujah for the no-hellites!

# Sailing the Straits

*False early conceptions darkened my childhood and youth. This faith in Universalism, during the years that I have believed it, has grown upon me, until it is the central thing in me. I do not engage in anything that is not, as I see it, the outcome of this faith. My later comprehension has given me a noble and abiding faith in human destiny.*

—Mary Ashton Rice Livermore

Scylla, a rock on the Italian coast, was personified by the ancients as a monster; Charybdis was a maelstrom off the Sicilian coast. The sailor's job was to navigate a safe course between the smooth, sheer rock of Scylla and the eddying whirlpool of Charybdis—a perilous strait where the sea forever spouted and roared and furious waves, mounting up, touched the very sky.

The Universalist journey, likewise, mandates our steering routes between the equally inviting, frightful obstacles of Scylla, or pessimism, which ever so quickly ossifies into cynicism, and Charybdis, representing the tantalizing shallows of optimism, or what Robert Bly calls "maddening cheerfulness." Facing these enticing dangers, one is reminded of Wolfgang Konisberg's (better known as Woody Allen) satirical assessment that more than any time in history, humankind faces a crossroads. One path leads to despair and utter hopelessness, the other to total extinction. Let us pray, he said, that we have the wisdom to choose correctly.

Let's take a closer look at Scylla, the rock, then Charybdis, the whirlpool.

Charles Schulz, in the comic strip *Peanuts*, illustrates the view of the pessimist in a conversation between the characters Linus and Charlie Brown. "Life is difficult, isn't it Charlie Brown?" "Yes, it is," Charlie replies. Linus continues, "But I've developed a new philosophy. . . I only dread one day at a time." In this era of mercurial change, pervasive boredom, and bone-deep anguish, the pessimist succumbs to dejection.

Pessimists look both ways on a one-way street. They believe that no human problem is truly solvable. They are self-fulfilling prophets of gloom, make that doom. They predict that next year is going to be catastrophic, and then, wittingly or unconsciously, they do everything imaginable to make sure it ends up that way. Pessimists migrate from the healthy posture of skepticism to the rigid, life-denying attitude of cynicism, therewith committing spiritual treason.

One of the qualities that impressed John Murray most about Rellyan theology in England, as he was evolving his own universalist sensibility, was the fact, as he put it "that they were not melancholy." He sensed that the religious vision, embodied by this British band of Universalists, resisted hopelessness. It was an uplifting, buoyant faith.

Although our globe has an abundance of card-carrying pessimists, it is also filled with mindless optimists walking the boulevards. As James Branch Cabell put it: "An optimist proclaims that we live in the best of all possible worlds, and the pessimist fears this is true."

Universalists would urge us to be vigilant while visiting the seductive, swirling undercurrents of Charybdis. Optimism is sneaky, eroding our critical faculties, enticing us into stagnation, or worse yet, arrogance. It arrives in the guise of high-sounding platitudes that promise to deliver bliss, covering life's existential anguish with coats of syrup. Optimists believe that George or Gertrude or God will take care of our soul-sized duties and responsibilities. We are lulled into lassitude.

For 200 years Universalists have known that the religious odyssey requires a virtue, sufficiently robust, like hope, to help us navigate our adventures, skillfully avoiding the rocks and whirlpools of existence. Hope is more durable than negativism and thicker than giddiness. Joining the company of Universalists, we steer our fragile yet sturdy crafts through the precarious straits between Scylla and Charybdis, fully aware of the dangers, imbued with a chastened sense of hopefulness.

# Let All Sorrows Ripen in Me

*We have become shabby hunters at spiritual bargain counters to find life's blessings at reduced prices. True worship stimulates this almost extinguished spark of idealism. The world has thrown ashes on the flame, but worship fans the dying embers lest they become utterly and forever cold. I fear more than any other thing the "terrible freezing up of the deep wells" of my spiritual life.*
— *Clarence Russell Skinner*

Universalist wisdom posits that hope and despair are like Siamese twins, inextricably linked, and when torn asunder, both wither. The French know this; the words *espoir* (hope) and *desespoir* (despair) are etymological kin. Therefore, the opposite reality of hope is never despair but diffidence, living without passion, unresponsive to the vicissitudes of human existence, mired in what the Middle Ages called the deadly sin of slothfulness. Despairing people may stumble, even wobble, but they remain grasping, full of kick.

Universalist tradition, despite its eternal hopefulness, has never invited the easy path. It has avoided the temptation to languish on our hindquarters, waiting to be rescued by external forces. Universalism declares that holiness and health are only achievable through facing the worst, dealing directly with despair. Universalism beckons earthlings to pay utmost homage to *this* universe, the only one we'll ever know, a universe beyond our creation, control, even comprehension, replete with inexplicable grandeur and ineradicable tragedy.

Hope is not a maudlin state of wishful thinking.

Hopers pay attention to the wrenching groans of earth. They acknowledge human complicity in creating a world of woe. As flawed yet resilient beings, hopers choose to sing lamentations, dance agonies, shout rage, descend into depths of despair on the pathway to empowerment. In these excerpts from two of her poems, "Of Grief" and "A Hard Death," Unitarian Universalist May Sarton describes her odyssey into the land of grief :

> There are some griefs so loud
> They could bring down the sky,
> And there are griefs so still
> None knows how deep they lie,
> Endured, never expended.
> There are old griefs so proud
> They never speak a word;
> They never can be mended.
> And these nourish the will
> And keep it iron-hard.
>
> We cannot save, be saved, but we can stand
> Before each presence with gentle heart and hand;
> Here in this place, in this time without belief,
> Keep the channels open for each other's grief;. . . .

It is crucial as carriers of hopefulness, nurtured in the Universalist faith, not to confuse sadness with depression. Sadness is a primal, ontological condition. It comes with the territory of being an awakened, sensitive human being. Depression occurs when we are trapped in self-pity or immobilized by despondency. Sadness is irremovable. Depression can be lessened, sometimes eliminated.

There will always be obstinate sadness during one's sojourn on this globe. We will mourn broken pledges, tortured bonds, devastated dreams, violated women, abused children, fallen men, ravaged earth. We are summoned as religious pilgrims to experience fully the pangs of such unavoidable, soul-shaking losses. The river of despair courses through our beings.

According to Robert Bly, hopers "rake the ashes," resisting the urge for quick release or instant enlightenment. Our lives, to be full and rounded, must marinate periodically in the juices of travail. As the Buddhist wisdom invites, "let all sorrows ripen in me."

Then, slowly yet inexorably, a realistic and seasoned hope, neither naive nor sentimental, emerges from the cultivated soil of our sorrow.

# The Stuff of Eternity

*I have planted a hope in my human heart. All that I can touch and see and say reminds me of my mortal limitations and cosmic insignificance. Every pain and pang tells me that I have but temporary possession of this dust that today is mine and me. I may die tomorrow. Surely, I shall not survive a hundred years. But my hope is larger than my limitations and braver than my body. Through my hope, I escape the remorseless march of time and the lack of meaning in material existence. Hopes do not die, and a hoping heart is of the stuff of eternity.*
—Albert Q. Perry

Universalism contends that human beings are ultimately known by our aspirations more than by our accomplishments. It is not living-room trophies but unquenchable longings of the spirit that measure our humanity. We are a people of the way, born not once or twice but again and again, forever.

Our Universalist ancestors have described this dynamic condition variously. L.B. Fisher wrote in 1921, "Universalists are often asked to tell where they stand. The only true answer to give to this question is that we do not stand at all, we move. Or we are asked to state our position. Again we can only answer that we are not staying to defend any position, we are on the march."

In 1785, Benjamin Rush talked about our country's destiny in process terms: "A belief has arisen that the American Revolution is over. This is so far from being the case that we have only finished the first act of the great drama."

Then Marion D. Shutter (1853-1939), who was the preeminent Universalist advocate of evolution, described our human becoming in this manner: "We have risen and not fallen; we did not begin perfect and deteriorate; but we began low and imperfect, and have been slowly but surely gaining in character and moral power. Everything points to the conclusion that we began at the very bottom, and have since been struggling painfully towards the summit."

So, hope signals a yearning for completion. We never reach fulfillment during our stay on earth, but we move ever forward, with occasional steps backwards or sideways. Hope arouses possibilities rather than fixating on goals. Hope sustains us along the tumultuous, twisting path, because it is propelled by deep-down resources of the soul. Unitarian Universalist Norman Cousins, twentieth-century proponent of revolutionary hopefulness, states it movingly:

> The case for hope has never rested on provable facts or rational assessment. Hope by its very nature is independent of the apparatus of logic. What gives hope its power is not the accumulation of demonstrable facts, but the release of human energies generated by the longing for something better. The capacity for hope is the most significant fact in life. It provides human beings with a sense of destination and the energy to get started. It enlarges sensitivities. It gives values to feelings as well as to facts.

Hopers stay on path, resisting those who would derail our quest. We keep traveling even when the specifics of destination are confusing or changed in midstream. Our spiritual yearning persists. Where there is no vision, the people perish. (Proverbs 29:18) Hope sustains our vision without dwelling on detailed results.

The obstructionists we hopers meet on our sacred journey are legion. I describe but a few.

Pessimists attempt to demoralize us by positing that life is hopelessly awful, oppressive, doomed. We receive the news, take it in stride, keep walking.

Optimists race by, trying to disrupt our deliberate pace. We wave to these well-intentioned speed merchants, yet remain on track, guided by stars beyond and light within.

Sentimentalists wish to lure us into retiring to a gorgeous, romantic village off the beaten path. We tender a friendly glance and saunter on.

Opportunists set up shop to peddle magic trinkets and relics for our trip. Choosing to travel simply, we decline additional tokens and push forward.

Faithful to the past, loving in the present, hopers forge tomorrows without number. For "hopes do not die, and a hoping heart is of the stuff of eternity."

# The Larger Hope

*Religion which is compartmentalized into narrow, specific confines of living is not worthy of the name religion. And if religious education must educate for all of life, it must do so in terms of what we believe as religious liberals. Our religious education is religious if we can help our children see the awe and wonder of the immensity of the universe of which they are a part, and yet sense an equal awe and wonder about the majesty of humankind.*
—Dorothy Spoerl (adapted)

Universalism affirms the Old Testament concept of salvation as a place of spaciousness and seconds Jesus' depiction "in my Father's house are many rooms. . . ." One of the most popular Universalist hymns echoes this same sentiment when it begins: "there's a wideness in God's mercy like the wideness of the sea. . . ." From its birth, Universalism has been a religious philosophy whose governing metaphor denotes breadth, size, expansiveness. At its truest, Universalism has been inclusive rather than restrictive in both spirit and structure.

Universalism represents the religious path (to employ Russell Miller's title) of "the larger hope," embracing all living things, engaging every area of existence, and enjoying the resources of the entire universe. As Universalist General Superintendent Robert Cummins stated in a 1943 address: "Any Universalism worthy of its name cannot recognize divisions between people on the basis of race or class or religion or nationality. . . . All are welcome . . . unitarian or trinitarian, white or colored, theist or humanist, so that whatever exclusion there may be is self-exclusion. A circumscribed Universalism is unthinkable."

Universalists hold that our humanity is judged by the size of our devotions and the stretch of our involvements. Consequently, the only hope large enough to heal the globe's brokenness will be one that pays homage to the gifts of women as well as men, children in addition to adults, and the marginalized alongside those in seats of privilege and power. A faith of the larger hope welcomes persons of diverse colors and classes, theologies and sexual orientations, ages and capacities. It aspires to be authentically, not artificially, inclusive.

As we turn the corner and head into the twenty-first century, the Universalist legacy challenges us to garner wisdoms from secular and sacred scriptures, to salute pioneers of justice and joy from every era, every culture, every corner of earth.

A child in our religious education program remarked once, when asked to describe the divine, that "God was fat." And the little children shall lead us in the ways of hope and courage, for any workable vision of deity must be sizeable enough to welcome a kaleidoscopic array of behaviors and beliefs, including those quite disparate from our own. Any God worth affirming must be fat, big, large enough to embrace all souls or none, and such a God exhorts us humans to be spacious of spirit in return.

Once we are grasped by the Universalist worldview, by its concept of a larger hope, it proves unbearable to rest satisfied with diminishing emotions, petty prejudices, and small-minded commitments. One cannot pursue the path of Universalism and long remain void of hope, riddled with cowardice, and stingy with love.

# Hopedale and Salubria

*My hope was too large and my economic judgment too small.*

—Adin Ballou

Scattered throughout the United States are cities whose names bespeak America's ambivalent pull toward attitudes of both pessimism and optimism.

A pessimistic map of the United States features such actual towns as Boring, Oregon; Troublesome, Colorado; Gripe, Arizona; Defiance, Iowa; Dismal, Tennessee; Bleak, West Virginia; and Purgatory, Maine. On the other side of the ledger, an optimistic touring guide highlights such villages as Progress, Oregon; Carefree, Arizona; Sweet, Idaho; What Cheer, Iowa; Sublime, Texas; Hi-Energy, Kentucky; Yum Yum, Tennessee; and Darling, Minnesota.

Three of the landmark places during the unfolding history of American Universalism have been Good Luck Point on Barnegat Bay, New Jersey, the harbor where John Murray docked after sailing across the Atlantic Ocean in 1770; Hopedale, Massachusetts, an intentional religious community established by Adin Ballou and committed to fostering peaceful nonresistance; and Salubria, Iowa, an experimental social commune founded by Abner Kneeland in 1839. Good Luck, Hopedale, and Salubria were all communities heralding the expectant vision of Universalism.

Murray's landing in the New World and pursuant establishment of Universalism on these shores is a well-chronicled passage. But, alas, Universalism would need to bank on more than Good Luck. Ballou and Kneeland, lesser acclaimed Universalists, suffered, like Murray, torment and tumult in the quest to fulfill their radical dreams. Good Luck would need to be joined by Hopedale and Salubria.

Adin Ballou (1803-1890) based his Hopedale Community on the principles of the Sermon on the Mount in the New Testament as well as the elemental convictions of Universalism. But because of economic hardships, his own overweaning aspirations and the moral frailties of followers, Hopedale failed to sustain itself as a viable community. Additionally, as biographer Clinton Lee Scott observed, "His theology was too conservative for the liberals and his sociology was too liberal for the conservatives."

Ballou remained an unrepentant radical, passionately devoted to reforming the world through pacifism, women's equality, temperance, and the abolition of slavery. He was a revolutionary ahead of both his time and devotees, and he grew dismayed at the unwillingness of Americans, including progressive Universalist comrades, to match Hopedale's ideals. Ballou was a principled Christian who declared, "We must not only preach but live by what we have received as truth or else renounce it honestly as impractical."

His formal ties with Universalism became strained, but his uncompromising commitment to peace-making and justice-building directly influenced Leo Tolstoi, Mahatma Gandhi and Martin Luther King, Jr., all of whom avowed their indebtedness to Adin Ballou.

Abner Kneeland's Universalist pilgrimage was even stormier than Ballou's. Kneeland was an opinionated, irascible leader who, in 1833, espoused an unorthodox "philosophical creed," even among Universalists. He wrote:

> I believe that the whole universe is NATURE, and that the word NATURE embraces the whole universe, and that God and Nature, so far as we can attach any rational idea to either, are perfectly synonymous terms. Hence I am not an Atheist, but a Pantheist; that is,

instead of believing there is no God, I believe that in the abstract, all is God; and that all power that is, is in God, and that there is no power except that which proceeds from God.

Kneeland's radical theology led to his dismissal from the Universalist ministerial fellowship. His 1845 sentencing to five years in the Massachusetts state prison was, fortunately, the last time a heresy trial happened in America. Kneeland was excluded from a denomination ostensibly committed to inclusion. His religious philosophy caused embarrassment to his sisters and brothers in faith, yet his banishment and ensuing imprisonment furnished a humiliating moment in the unusually tolerant history of Universalism. Universalism may have believed in an all-loving God, but its human adherents were imperfect, and, upon occasion, unduly judgmental.

Kneeland later founded a utopian community in Iowa that he named Salubria, where members earned their livelihood as farmers and spent free hours addressing religious and social concerns. Salubria literally refers to a place favorable to one's well-being—in sum, a healthy and holy location. With his death, the Salubria community waned, but its spirit and influence lingered.

As Ballou's pacifism paved the way for peace activists in ensuing generations, Kneeland's pantheism opened the door for broader understandings of the divine among Universalist descendants.

These two often-thorny truth-tellers and doers, Ballou and Kneeland, pricked the conscience of Universalism and punctured its illusions. Grateful for their courage, we stand beholden, readier to risk today our own versions of theology and social witness.

# Happiness and Holiness Are Inseparable

*And I took it so to heart that I believed my happiness would be incomplete while one creature remained miserable.*
—George de Benneville

The only salvation worth having is communal, extended to everyone. Western religion, in its excessive narcissism, remains largely preoccupied with the query "Are *you* saved?" rather than "Are *we* saved?" Universalism claims that God will travel, if necessary, to the ends of the earth and the recesses of hell to make peace with offspring of the cosmos. Ultimately, there is no escape from the loving caress of the Creator. The final clubhouse of souls, states sound Universalist doctrine, will include the outcastes of history, the "anawim" (the little, poor, helpless ones among us), and plenty of folks whom productive, respectable types seldom welcome into our earthly clans. In sum, an open-handed God will triumph over the tight-fisted ways of humanity.

The Hebrew term for hope has the bedrock meaning of "to twist" or "to twine" and is etymological kin to the word *kivin* for spiderweb—that fragile, resilient network of tiny, interweaving threads. Hopers celebrate wholeheartedly "the interdependent web of all existence of which we are a part." Humans add to the fabric even as we are created by it. Being connected to all of life, hopers, as Unitarian Universalist Bernard Loomer emphasized in his relational theology, are charged "to heal and strengthen that part of the cosmic web where we nest."

T.S. Eliot refers to hell as the place "where nothing connects with nothing." Shattered family covenants are hell. Nationalistic sentiments exploding into war cause untold hell. Ecological havoc wreaks hell. Vacuous work, frantic addictions, consuming loneliness—"where nothing connects with nothing"—result in living hells. One recalls the summons from Ecclesiastes (9:4) in the Old Testament: "for to those who are joined to all the living, there is hope." When we are self-centered, we receive temporary gratification, but never enduring hope, which arrives in its fullness only when we dare to risk living beyond privatism, partialism, and provincialism.

John Murray re-enters our dialogue, proclaiming with fervor: "Give them, not Hell, but hope . . ." and once again our marching orders are unmistakably clear. As committed, albeit blemished, carriers of the Universalist message, we are urged to diminish the hell and enhance the hope where we live, move, and have our beings, beginning today.

Universalists believed that just as misery and sin were irrevocably connected, so also happiness and holiness were inseparable. Humans could reach the former via the latter. We would find satisfaction by living virtuously. Only the path of goodness could "happify" us, to use the charming eighteenth-century Universalist term.

The call to incarnate happy, holy lives is poignantly conveyed in the ruminations of Betty Mills, a contemporary Unitarian Universalist traveler:

> When I am an old woman, I shall wear mostly jeans and T-shirts that say outrageous things. I will quit cooking Mother's Day dinner and cross out sexist words with red ink in library books and leave parties when someone tells a sick joke on gays . . . but maybe I ought to practice a little now? So people who know me are not too shocked and surprised when suddenly I am old and start to wear T-shirts.

Who we are to be, we are now becoming. We would all do well to "practice a little now."

# Grand Possibilities Are All Before Us

*From the moment I believed in Universalism, it was a matter of course that I was to preach it.*
—Augusta Jane Chapin

Augusta Jane Chapin (1836-1905), a painfully shy and sensitive child, evolved into one of Universalism's superlative preachers and reformers. Deeply dismayed as a young adult by the problem of eternal punishment, Chapin reasoned her way through to the Universalist affirmation that all persons were redeemable. Persuaded of her call to ministry, she spread the Universalist gospel with unswayable passion. Unitarian Universalist historian David Johnson rightly calls Chapin "an indefatigable evangelist for Universalism."

She served forty years as a circuit-riding preacher especially in the Midwest. In 1893, Chapin was awarded the honorary degree of Doctor of Divinity by Lombard University, the first granted a woman in this country.

Augusta was also an activist in the fields of temperance, women's rights, and education, standing stalwart among Universalist champions of justice. She was a thoroughgoing protestor, a prophetic voice who testified on behalf of her values and visions. In response to the provocative query, "If you were on trial for being a Unitarian Universalist, would there be enough evidence to convict you?" the verdict on Augusta Jane Chapin would be a resounding yes. She was guilty of being an indefatigable evangelist, a hope-filled reformer, a holy activist.

Augusta Jane Chapin comes to mind whenever I read

the passage from fellow Universalist Clarence Skinner, composed in 1940: "We need spiritual giants in the earth who dare to break the shackles of the past; creative, onward-looking pioneers, who dare to go forward." Chapin marched forward as a witness for Universalism in an era of superstition, prejudice, and fear.

It was an arduous, often agonizing, trek for women to create, then sustain, a viable ministry in the nineteenth century. In the face of opposition within and beyond Universalism, Chapin was dauntless, stubbornly refusing to succumb to the clutches of apathy or cynicism, an exemplar of steady hopefulness. Near the end of her life, Universalism was blessed as a movement with as many as seventy women preachers.

One hundred years ago, in 1893, Chapin was chosen to address the prestigious, overflowing throng at the World's Parliament of Religions. With stirring words she extended the hand of collegiality to all the men and women congregated during that historic convention in Chicago:

> We are still in the dawn, the very early dawn, of the new era. Its grand possibilities are all before us. We are assembled in this great Parliament to look for the first time in each other's faces and speak to each other our best and our truest words. I can only add my word of earnest and heartfelt greetings to those who have gone before, and welcome you, my brothers, from every land and of many faiths, who have wrought so long, so grandly, and so well, in accordance with the wisdom high heaven has given you. And I welcome you, my sisters, who have come with beating hearts and high hopes and reverent purposes to this great feast to participate, not only in this Parliament, but in the great congresses which are associated with it, to behold that an Isabella of Spain had a prophetic vision—she beheld not only a new world, but also a new

future—an emancipated and intelligent womanhood [applause] and a strengthened religion to bless the world. I welcome you to the fulfillment of her grand vision.

In 1993, as sisters and brothers advancing on a common venture, we gather "with beating hearts and high hopes and reverent purposes," aspiring to build a world of enduring gender justice and joy.

May we be as indefatigable in that quest as our Universalist sister, Augusta Jane Chapin, was in her era.

# Universalism Lives On . . .

*I have asked contemporary Universalist laity and religious professionals to share their thoughts on hope, courage, and the love of God. Here are some of their contributions.*

---

In the attic of my home in Maine, I once discovered a yellowed letter written by a man in response to the death of a relative. "She died happy. She was a Universalist." Dying happy is not one of my life goals, but I was reminded of an empowering lesson I had learned in my Universalist church school. It is best expressed by the poet Milton: "The mind is its own place and in itself can make a Hell of Heaven, a Heaven of Hell." Universalism is a matter of spirit more than a theology. It is a generous spirit searching for the good in all things and expecting the best from others and oneself. I can live happily with that!

—Drusilla Cummins

---

I cannot know the joy of faith discovered. The elation experienced by others who find their home in our liberal religion is unknown to me. For me, the faith has been there always—a heritage of centuries come and gone.

My ancestors were Huguenots. Denied the right to own and practice their faith, they left their Alsacian homes for England, easily plying their trade as silk merchants. Great Britain, however, offered no sanctuary for their religious beliefs. Continuing the journey, their sons and daughters sought the dream of freedom in the new world, following pilgrims and puritans to the shores of North America. The dream was yet again deferred as they discovered that intolerance had not been washed away in the cold Atlantic seas.

Not alone, however, companions with shared aspirations were found, and together they continued the adventure to found a free religious community in Quaker Rhode Island. Later generations followed in the Quaker faith, carrying it north to yet unsettled areas until, over two-hundred years after the Alsacian exodus, the Universalist connection was made in a tiny town in Maine. From Huguenot to Quaker to Universalist, the free thought flowed through generations of my family. It is now four hundred years of family history—of saving a faith for me and my descendants. It is a heritage I treasure more than there is any means to measure.

No, I cannot know the joy of faith discovered. But I can hold out this heritage to share. For it belongs to all of us—to own, to cherish, to serve as the foundation for a faith that develops, evolves, but keeps free thought as its ground for growth.

—Barbara Mosher DeWolfe

An insight I have learned from my years in ministry comes from my own Universalist theology. It concerns the idea that a loving God does not condemn anyone to eternal damnation. And when I apply this concept here on earth, I feel it is my responsibility to work for inclusion in all contexts.

I always have felt that ostracism of any kind is a hell on earth, imposed by those who have the power to control through their own sense of superiority. Yet I believe that every person, no matter how evil, has the seed of goodness within. And no person, because of his or her past, must forever be alienated from the trust and goodwill of the community.

—Charles Gaines

I suppose I was ten or eleven years old when my Grandfather King shook his finger at me and said, "Remember Peggy, you belong to the NO HELL Church." I don't know whether his concept of "no hell" was of a literal heaven or not, but that doesn't matter. He spoke with such conviction and lived his life in such a way that what was communicated to me, and has stayed with me, is an unshakable hope for the future.

This is not a passive hope, nor one that denies personal or global tragedy, but one that requires us to keep working for a better future for ourselves and others. This is the essence of Universalism for me, hope and its corollary, good works, founded on a theology of love and reason.

—Margaret K. Gooding

# Courage

# Benevolence

*Conduct is three-fourths of life. The present life is the great pressing concern.*
—P.T. Barnum

The English poet and playwright Ben Jonson claimed that courage was the primary virtue, since without bravery we were incapable of demonstrating all the other values. Cowards remain in the dugout, never entering the playing fields of existence, where challenges are faced and uniforms dirtied. If truth be told, most of our ethical careers are checkered stories and resemble Woody Allen's analysis: "I'm not a coward, and I'm not a hero. I'm somewhere in the middle."

Give them hope *and* courage. These two virtues are inextricably yoked. Hopers are not mere dreamers, waiting passively. They are encouragers, doers who risk their visions. A theology of hope must finally translate into an ethic of resistance. If we cannot utterly reverse the evils of existence, we can unceasingly resist them.

On the practical level, then, hopers know that the best antidote to desperation is action, not frenzied busyness, but vigorous deeds that feed one's own spirit while simultaneously nourishing humanity. Hopers also assert that the only way to beat self-preoccupation and greed is by giving generously to life-engendering causes.

Courage comes from the French word "coeur" for heart, so brave persons are blessed with an abundant supply of heartiness. They discern when it is prudent to flee or confront the trials of existence. Courageous persons walk the tightrope between adventurousness and foolhardiness. In

*Moby Dick*, by Unitarian Herman Melville, the chief mate Starbuck says to his crew: "I will have no one in my boat who is not afraid of a whale." Melville writes: "By this Starbuck seemed to mean not only was the most reliable and useful courage that which arises from the fair estimation of the encountered peril, but that an utterly fearless person is a far more dangerous comrade than a coward."

Courage does not always require immediate, harsh heroics. Indeed, it should calm rather than inflame the mind. Courage is able to be patient as well as prompt.

For Universalists, the bond between hope and courage was sustained by the conviction that they were unreservedly loved by God, hence, secure in their todays and hopeful about their tomorrows. This underlying assurance gave them incentive to pass God's love on to their neighbors. From the opening Universalist convention in Philadelphia in 1790, the call to courageous social reform was clarion. Caring for humanity was the Universalist way of thanking their Creator. Universalist author Elmo Robinson reports:

> As the years passed, gatherings of Universalists devoted far more time to social reform than to heavenly discourse. No great evil of those days escaped their attention: the intemperance that is now known as alcoholism, the emerging racial problem after emancipation, treatment of criminals, liberation of women. There was speech after speech, of course, yet there was also action.

Universalists were a pious, reflective clan but rarely paralyzed by inordinate navel-gazing. They were mystical reformers whose hope invariably converted into deeds of prophetic witness. Benevolence is the overarching principle of Universalism that activated their myriad social reforms. It literally refers to acts of kindness and the practice of magnanimity. The Universalists were a benevolent people, whose goodwill resulted in compassionate behavior. Grounded in God's love, they were motivated to love those in need. As a benevolent community, they aspired to make the world more beautiful and just during their earthly sojourn.

Universalists were frequently perceived by mainline Protestant and Catholic historians as recommending, even displaying, an opportunistic pathway to heaven. This assessment of Universalists wrongfully assumed that saved human beings would fritter their lives away in depravity rather than service. Abraham Lincoln, after being censured by evangelist Peter Cartwright for attending the Universalist Church in Urbana, Illinois, was reported to have said: "Parson, I used to think that it took the smartest person to uphold and defend Universalism, but now I think differently, for I believe it to be the easiest doctrine to defend that I have yet heard."

Lincoln disclosed a partial truth. The Universalist mission was easy to state, even defend, but most difficult to incarnate. Its message of hope, courage, and the love of God was simple and clear but arduous to put into practice, for it required that human beings reply to God's unconditional love with abounding compassion and caregiving of our own. No easy task whatsoever.

Universalists were motivated neither by fear of hell nor guilt of clergy but by love. The Universalist prophets and pioneers honored in these pages were exemplary but flawed. They didn't accomplish everything they set out to do, but achieved one more thing each day for justice and mercy than the day before. They were morally courageous women and men, not perfect ones. They didn't walk on water but searched for the rocks beneath, planted themselves, then dove into the depths when cries of need were sounded.

In closing, we dare not forget the courageous work of Universalist P.T. Barnum, who was more than a scintillating entertainer. He was a morally concerned civic leader of considerable fortitude who, before he created the Barnum and Bailey circus, served as Mayor of Bridgeport, Connecticut, where he battled union discrimination against African-Americans and joined in the battle against prostitution.

A benevolent person.

# Let Love Continue

*Let love continue. If we agree in love, there is no disagreement that can do us any injury; but if we do not, no other agreement can do us any good. Let us keep a secret guard against the enemy that sows discord among us. Let us endeavor to keep the unity of spirit in the bonds of peace.*
—Hosea Ballou

Although there is no nobler summation of the Universalist message than Ballou's invitation to "let love continue," in actuality, Hosea Ballou could be downright recalcitrant and testy, a controversial figure. But, then again, John Murray was considered imperious and Thomas Whittemore, pugnacious. So Universalism represents a tradition of imperfect individuals, not faultless paragons of virtue. The fact that Universalist history contained quarrelsome personalities in its ranks makes it a more human, compelling heritage.

To "let love continue" is no minor accomplishment. Loving in word and deed, loving friend and foe, loving amid conflict demands utmost courage. Universalists would concur with Martin Luther King, Jr. who said, "The ultimate measure of human beings is not where we stand in moments of comfort and convenience, but where we stand at times of challenge and controversy."

Universalists have been prominent throughout American history for tackling the major socio-ethical challenges of their day, often assuming unpopular stands. According to Russell Miller, Universalists in 1857 addressed no less than forty areas of prophetic concern, including economic and domestic relations (slavery, wages, marriage, women's rights), international relations (war, commerce, foreign slave trade, colonization, conflict of races), social institutions and habits (temperance, education, politics and laws, amusements, the poor, dress, food), and offenders and irresponsible or unfortunate persons (capital punishment, juvenile offenders, dueling, gambling, insanity, deaf and dumb).

This small but mighty band of religious pilgrims known as Universalists confronted, with compassionate reasonableness, the social ills and demons of their day. They never shirked their responsibility to translate theological resolve into ethical action. Universalism was an applied, not merely espoused, religion.

Yet the Universalist reach in social witness usually exceeded its grasp. Accomplishments fell short of stated goals. This prophetic faith had moments in history when it failed to mount concerted social witness, hampered by its overweaning individualism. Honorable Universalists were also known to hold markedly different moral positions on social evils, whether the issue was abolition, women's rights, criminal justice reform, or pacifism.

There were even periods of internal rancor. From the 1830s to the 1850s, one of Universalism's feisty mini-schisms transpired between the restorationists, who believed that a limited period of suffering (Elhanan Winchester claimed 50,000 years of purgatory would suffice) in the next life was in order before the final restoration, and the ultra-Universalists, who believed that upon physical death, all were ushered into heavenly peace with no future punishment in store. This was a theological controversy that pitted Universalists against one another, but ultimately mutual respect prevailed, and they proceeded onward as a unified movement.

Universalism was a faith that encouraged people to be true to one's own conscience while honoring that of one's neighbor. Universalism exhorted its disciples, especially in times of strain and disagreement, to stay close and caring, to remain in conversation, to heed the counsel of their exemplar, Hosea Ballou, "to keep the unity of the spirit in the bonds of peace."

# Agitators for Equality

*Each true life, whether public or private, which any woman of the century has lived, goes to make up the character and glory of the land and the age; and every high soul rejoices in the welfare of her native land, whether her name be found on the scroll of its famous women or not.*

—Phebe A. Hanaford

The feminist pioneers of the Universalist movement in America have furnished us with a hopeful, courageous legacy. Their abounding wisdom and dedication dare not be forgotten. Those of us committed to the cause of gender justice today follow in the footsteps of our Universalist agitators for equality.

In Judith Sargent Murray's essay entitled "On the Equality of the Sexes," she wrote: "Yes, . . . our souls are by nature equal to yours; the same breath of God animates, enlivens and invigorates us. . . ." Murray (1751-1820) was a feminist essayist, poet, and commentator of considerable note. Judith was ambitious on her own, while remaining energetic on behalf of her husband, John. Among her admiring subscribers were John Adams, George and Martha Washington, and Benjamin Franklin.

Olympia Brown (1835-1926) was the first woman ordained by denominational (Universalist) sanction in America. In addition to serving as a parish minister, Brown was a devoted partner, mother, and unrelenting advocate of women's suffrage. In an epoch when women were caricatured as weak and illness-prone, Olympia Brown's life was one of remarkable stamina and undiminished bravery:

> In over ten years as a pastor, Brown "never yet was absent from an engagement or suspended labor on account of sickness." While travelling in Kansas from July to November 1867 on behalf of women's suffrage, she delivered no less than 205 discourses, and experienced no ill effects. The author of a contemporary account of Brown's travels in Kansas called attention to the fact that she had "great physical power of endurance, lately speaking two or three times each day, in the hottest weather, travelling from twenty to fifty miles each day, with only an average of about four hours sleep, and her speeches from one to two hours in length, without apparently the least fatigue, and weighing only ninety-one pounds avoirdupois."

Another Universalist minister who labored tirelessly in the vineyards of equality for women was Phebe Ann Coffin Hanaford (1829-1921), a contemporary of Olympia Brown. Reared as a Quaker, Phebe was inspired early on by women preachers like her cousin Lucretia Mott. Hanaford displayed moral precocity as a child when, at eight years of age, she signed the temperance pledge and at thirteen wrote for the press. Phebe served Universalist congregations from 1868 until 1891, officiated at the funeral services of her cohorts Elizabeth Cady Stanton and Susan B. Anthony, and died at the age of 92. It is heartening to note the number of Universalist feminists who stayed vigorous into their nineties.

In her splendid book *Daughters of America*, Hanaford saluted the contributions of an astounding array of female poets, scientists, reformers, physicians, business leaders (such as Universalist Lydia Pinkham), lawyers, agriculturalists, historians, and others.

Lesser known, but other worthy Universalist women need to be remembered as well, lest their testimonies fade in anonymity. Women ministers such as Maria Cook (1779-1835), who was ridiculed as an eccentric woman; Sally Barnes Dunn (1783 1858), who purportedly could preach as good a sermon in ten minutes as most ministers could in an hour; and Lydia A. Jenkins, who was the first woman to deliver a commencement address in 1859 at Lombard University and serve in a full-time parish ministry in Clinton, New York, with her husband.

It is also significant that among Universalists from 1793 to 1993, there have been a number of profeminist men, such as Horace Greeley and Daniel Livermore, who courageously struggled within themselves and society against the patronizing attitudes toward and outright oppression of women.

Mary Livermore (1820-1905) certainly earned the title granted her by Great Britain as "America's Queen of the Platform," because she spoke in Universalist congregations as a layperson at least half of the Sundays as well as lecturing at home and abroad. As Clinton Lee Scott reports: "Her booking agents warned her against dealing with controversial matters. She listened but went her own way, speaking on the most divisive questions of the day—women's equality with men, the liquor problem, suffrage, the double standard in sexual morality and marital relations."

Her most famous lecture, delivered over 800 times across America, was entitled "What Shall We Do with Our Daughters?" Livermore was a consummate writer as well, penning voluminously for Universalist publications. It comes as no surprise, therefore, that she established a periodical primarily dedicated to women's suffrage, appropriately called *The Agitator*.

Toward the end of her life, Mary Rice Ashton Livermore wrote: "I congratulate women that their long struggle for freedom, knowledge, opportunity, and the rights of human nature is nearly ended, and that the day is close at hand when it shall be as good a thing to be born a girl as to be born a boy." She didn't live to see women's suffrage become a complete reality, but her words and deeds kept the vision alive. It should be acknowledged that even progressive Universalists were torn on the issue of women's political enfranchisement. The march toward full egalitarianism was a halting one in the nineteenth century and remains so in the waning moments of ours as well.

    Hope and courage are essential virtues to be incarnated at every turn, to combat the sexual discrimination women face in the continuing quest for gender justice and joy. Our Universalist feminist "agitators" for equality summon us to join their struggle.

# Patriots, One and All

*The wish to promote the reputation of my own sex, and do something for my own country, was among the earliest mental emotions I can recollect.*
—Sarah Josepha Hale

Unitarians and Universalists are united in one religious association with differing theological beliefs and political commitments. Our eternal challenge is to celebrate our sense of unity, not uniformity, amidst our wondrous diversity. In the 200-year sweep of Universalist history, the pluralism of patriotic stances is strikingly evident.

Sarah Josepha Hale (1788-1879), widely admired Universalist author, social reformer, and long-time editor of *Godey's Lady's Book*, worked unflaggingly for educational and professional opportunities for women. She also pursued patriotic ventures, being largely responsible for making Thanksgiving a national holiday in America and raising monies to make permanent national monuments of Boston's Bunker Hill and Mt. Vernon. She was a loyalist to her beloved country.

Adin Ballou evolved from a chaplain of the Massachusetts militia to a full-blown radical peacemaker who traced his war resistance to the New Testament. Although Ballou was a pioneering pacifist among Universalists, there were others in ensuing years who suffered as well for their convictions, such as Harold Scott who spent a night in jail and L. Griswold Williams who lost his pastorate in western New York.

Daniel Bragg Clayton, a Universalist pastor from the South who served the Confederate army in the Civil War, was moved in 1889 to exclaim: "The sober truth about war is, that it will never cease till the nations become thoroughly imbued with the genuine principles and spirit of Universalism."

Perhaps the most decorated patriot of all was Clara Barton (1821-1912), founder of the American Red Cross. She labored courageously for three years, following the cannon into the midst of blazing gunfire. Barton served her country as an "Angel of the Battlefield," bringing comfort and solace to the wounded even as she endured incredible hardships on the field of duty. Until the day she died, in her 91st year, Clara Barton continued as a servant at her country's behest, a deliverer of mercy to those suffering amid flood or fire, earthquake, or starvation.

These Universalists exemplified distinct versions of patriotic service. They were all loyalists to their homeland and wore their patriotism honorably. Their understanding of patriotism encompassed the following principles.

First, patriots participate. They are activists. They serve their country, abroad or at home. Authentic patriots never enjoy the luxury of standing on the sidelines or sitting in the stands; they cannot be spectators. Patriots send letters to the soldiers or to the administration. Patriots extend relief support to victims on both sides of any war. Patriots participate in prayer vigils and protest marches. Patriots hear speeches but, more importantly, risk making their own.

Second, patriots carry on a "lover's quarrel" with their country, to use Robert Frost's phrase. They are willing to criticize their homeland when it falls short of humane visions, to congratulate it when it embodies peace with justice, and to comfort it when it needs genuine consolation. Patriots don't love mindlessly or obey submissively. No country worth its honor wants slaves and conformists. Patriots don't want their country to be great because of possessions or conquests. They want their country to be marked by a citizenry committed to intellectual freedom and moral justice.

Third, patriots are bilateral in their devotion, maintaining allegiance to both homeland and globe. They are not interested in national superiority but in international solidarity. For them, human sovereignty always transcends national sovereignty.

Finally, patriots follow their consciences. Whatever form patriotism might take, be it service in the military or protest on the streets, or both at different times, patriotism needs to be grounded in conscience, the best guideline for moral behavior with which humans are blessed. Patriots don't receive the words of the generals, dissenters, or commentators as ultimate truth. Rather, they seriously search the depths of their own consciences, believing that in a democracy, we must all be experts on issues of freedom and justice, peace and war.

Patriots, in our faith tradition, would concur with the sentiment of Unitarian Universalist prophet Stephen Fritchman: "Today's surgeons can transplant hearts, kidneys, and other human organs; but no man or woman in the health sciences can yet transplant a conscience. Feed and care for your conscience as you do your brain; neither can be replaced."

# Circuit Riders

*I have written everything from a sermon to a song and done everything from making sorghum molasses in a log cabin on a prairie to preaching three times a Sunday in the city of London.*
—Caroline Augusta White Soule

Universalists were conflicted about spreading their good news. Their congregations were fiercely independent, loosely organized, somewhat provincial. Yet, blessed with an uplifting message, Universalists could hardly help but be evangelists, even if low-key ones. Relying on circuit riders to do missionary work, some Universalist clergy traveled from congregation to congregation—organizing, speaking, trouble-shooting, and shoring up when necessary.

Two remarkable Universalists with evangelistic zeal were Quillen Hamilton Shinn (1845-1907) and Caroline Soule (1824-1903). The former worked on American soil, while the latter was Universalism's first foreign missionary. They both labored inexhaustibly to extend the Universalist gospel of abiding hope, contagious courage, and God's all-encompassing love. The Universalist story was seldom sensational but always steady, a gospel of stirring possibilities.

Quillen Hamilton Shinn, the spearhead in establishing domestic missions from Nebraska to New England to the South in post-Civil War America, organized summer conferences and labored as continental Universalist missionary for the Young People's Christian Union. Shinn was described variously as "the wandering nomad of Universalism"; "St. Paul"; and, most affectionately, as "the grasshopper missionary," because he bounded from one location to another.

Deeply dedicated to the Universalist faith and possessed of both exceptional organizational skill and an exuberant personality, Shinn became a circuit rider par excellence. His motto was: "There is no hell for any of us to fear outside of ourselves." Additionally, he put in long hours: "In the two years of 1904 and 1905 Shinn delivered 453 sermons in twenty-two states; travelled more than 38,000 miles, an estimated 900 of them on horseback or on foot; and assisted in building seven churches, five of which he dedicated."

One of Shinn's goals, never fully realized, was to commission every Universalist minister to serve a term as a field missionary. The resurgence of commitment to extension efforts in this closing decade of the twentieth century would have warmed the cockles of Quillen Hamilton Shinn's heart.

Caroline Soule was born into a Universalist family and married a Universalist minister, Henry Soule, who died prematurely in 1852, leaving his wife with minimal funds and five young children. Despite shouldering enormous burdens, Soule emerged as Universalist's foremost evangelist, publishing two million pages of denominational literature and sending it over the entire world.

But her bravest missionary venture would occur in Scotland where Soule organized a Scottish Universalist Convention, participated in the dedication of their first congregation, and, in 1880, was officially ordained as the minister of St. Paul's Universalist Church. She became an unusually beloved pastor in a land where a feminist presence was utterly foreign. Two years after her retirement, she wrote: "I was always tired, for there was never a chance to rest . . . but fatigue in the cause of Universalism is infinitely better than inaction, apathy, indolence."

John Murray immigrated to American shores in the late stages of the eighteenth century, being persuaded to stay and preach the Universalist message of hope, courage, and the love of God. Caroline Soule returned the favor a century later, crossing the ocean, and taking Universalism back to Great Britain.

In 1993, as yet another fresh century comes into focus, the UUA Director of Extension Charles Gaines has thrown down the gauntlet to our liberal religious movement, challenging us to become 250,000 strong by the year 2000.

Are we willing intentionally to spawn our faith? Do we have a hopeful, courageous gospel that can serve, possibly even save, the planet? Will we hide our light under a bushel or place it on a lampstand for all to see?

John Murray's exhortation haunts us still: "You may possess only a small light but uncover it, let it shine, use it in order to bring more light and understanding to the hearts and minds of men and women."

# Reluctant Reformers for Racial Justice

*We believe it to be inconsistent with the union of the human race in a common Savior, and the obligations to mutual and universal love, which flow from that union, to hold any part of our fellow creatures in bondage.*
—Benjamin Rush

There were indications of commitment to racial justice in the formative days of Universalism. One of the original twelve members of the first Universalist congregation, founded in 1770 in Gloucester, Massachusetts, was signed Gloucester Dalton, African. In the 1790s Benjamin Rush was a leader in establishing the first antislavery society in America. Mary Livermore, a native New Englander and prominent Universalist lay leader, spent time in southern Virginia, experiencing the slavery system first-hand, and became "a pronounced abolitionist, accepting from no one any apology for slavery."

Universalism claimed that God loved all creatures equally and that freedom was to be distributed universally. As Universalist social activist Clarence Skinner stated:

> The Universalist idea of God is that of a universal, impartial, immanent spirit whose nature is love. . . . This is no tribal deity of ancient, divisive civilization, this is no God of the nation or of a chosen people, but the democratic creator of the solid, indivisible world of rich and poor, black and white, good and bad, strong and weak, Jew and Gentile, bond and free; such a faith

is as much a victory for the common people as was the passage of the Fourteenth Amendment to the Constitution.

Yet the record of both Universalists and Unitarians, with respect to racial sensitivity and inclusion, has been marked by high intentions and checkered achievements. Russell Miller summarizes the uneven response of Universalism to racial oppression:

> After all, as the editors of the *Universalist Miscellany* told their readers in 1846, belief in the [kinship] of all people was "one of the distinguishing excellencies of Universalism." The world was in reality one great family; "however remote we may live from each other, however different may be our complexions, we are all [brothers and sisters]. . . ." But the historical fact is that Universalists were no more able than their contemporaries in other denominations to translate into immediate effective action an ideal by abolishing an institution that had become so inextricably interwoven into the fabric of the entire nation and which involved as many complexities and contradictions as slavery.

Generally, Universalist reformers were moderate rather than revolutionary on racial justice matters. They were often ambivalent, occasionally silent. Nonetheless, their bedrock principles of hope, courage, and a loving God would keep the issue of racial justice prominently on the agenda and hearts of practicing Universalists.

Let us revisit a few of the Universalist-related episodes and witnesses in the struggle for racial equality in America.

Near the close of the nineteenth century, African-American Universalist minister Joseph Fletcher Jordan (1863-1929) established a Universalist school in Suffolk, Virginia, which served for more than seven decades as a community center for the educational needs primarily of black youngsters, yet open to students of "all colors, sizes and ages."

After Jordan died, his daughter Annie Willis assumed directorship for some 48 years of the Neighborhood House. The center continued to reflect her father's unyielding commitment to service and fairness: "Every child must know her or his worth." Willis expanded its social outreach efforts, including a medical clinic, then a Headstart program.

W. E. B. DuBois declared that color would present the most intransigent, divisive social problem for twentieth-century America. His prediction has unfortunately proven true. Whiteness still denotes the dominant, normative culture on this continent. Unitarian Universalist Whitney Young challenged Americans to combat racial prejudice in his book *Beyond Racism*: "The racism that pervades our society and influences the behavior of individuals and institutions alike must yield to the demands for justice and freedom. Together, blacks and whites can move our country beyond racism and create for the benefit of all of us an Open Society, one that assures freedom, justice and full equality for all."

As the twentieth century nears its conclusion, another Unitarian Universalist, Bill Jones, minister and professor of Black Studies at Florida State University, describes the pervasive, insidious neo-racism abroad in our land: "America is racist and has been from its start. The racist cancer is as strong today as ever, but we feel it has diminished or vanished because we have camouflaged racism in order to perpetuate it. To change the system, whites must be willing to redistribute power and relinquish privilege."

The beat goes on. The vision remains. As a predominantly white denomination, we struggle to avoid both alienation and assimilation on the road to creating a multicultural society. Authentic pluralism that honors the various ethnicities and races of North America is the only reality hopeful, courageous, and loving enough to serve the cause of enduring racial justice.

In her biography of Whitney Young, Nancy J. Weiss recounts the graveside tribute for Young in Kentucky that President Nixon attended. After the burial service, a widely circulated photograph depicting Young's wife, Margaret, leaning close to Nixon, carried the following caption: "Mrs. Young embracing the President after the service." Margaret later revealed that she was in fact whispering to the President that she fully expected him to make progress on the high-sounding racial justice commitments he had made to her husband in the December meeting with the cabinet. She was challenging rather than hugging the President.

That challenge remains before us today. As a religious movement we are urged to bear witness to our lofty ideal of the inherent worth and dignity of every person. Racial justice is not a short-term cause but a life-long quest for Unitarian Universalists. Perhaps it is time to outgrow our reluctance as reformers.

# Lovers Tossed by These Difficult Times

*Know that the love which blooms inside you is stronger than fear, for people who love find strength they didn't know they had. Know that the love inside you is stronger than illness, for people who love hang in when physical health is gone. And know that love is indeed stronger than death, for people who love are like stones tossed into a pool. The circles of love radiate out and echo back long after the stone has come to rest on the bottom. So remember your love as a source of strength; remember who you are: lovers tossed by these difficult times.*
—Mark Mosher DeWolfe

In a reform-focused heritage such as Universalism, its history is generously sprinkled with activist anecdotes. But bravery comes in various guises. Courageous persons are spiritually balanced, receiving as well as giving succor.

Learning how to receive love is exceptionally difficult for hard-driving, compassionate Universalist types, especially ministers ordained to servanthood. Yet welcoming help from outsiders is a keen reminder that we humans are never self-sufficient and that utter graciousness resides at the heart of reality.

Unitarian Universalist minister Greta Crosby shares her theology of grace: "I am not fussy about forms or spiritual geography. Whether help comes from the outside or inside, by praying or willing, is not important. What is important is that help can come!"

Universalism isn't fussy either. It knows from experience that transformative help arrives from within and beyond, above and below, heaven and earth, from transcendent as well as immanent sources. In cultivating our interior soil with song and stillness, prayer and waiting, we prepare the way for life-nourishing comfort. Universalism shouts from the housetops: help can come, hope is real, hallelujah!

Mark Mosher DeWolfe, a lifelong Universalist, in the waning months of his struggle with AIDS, demonstrated the receiving posture of fortitude. He surrendered increasingly to the caring embrace of his faith community. An openly gay minister, DeWolfe was called to a Canadian congregation in 1981. When he was diagnosed with AIDS in 1986, then became ill, DeWolfe bravely invited the very same parishioners whom he had served so faithfully to become his caregivers. Mark recalls the shift in congregational life as the overall ministry was democratized among the membership:

> By sharing leadership we became a much better partnership, and our church is a much rounder, more complete place. Hard to learn also was to let the congregation love me in its own way. . . . Loving me in their own way meant more than just letting them bring me casseroles when I was too ill to cook. It meant letting them worry even when the worry was distressing them. . . . Just as they were willing to take the original risk in calling an openly gay minister, they have chosen to take the risk of remaining faithful in the face of death. They could have pensioned me off right away, removing me and the stigma of my disease from the church. They could even have done that in the name of compassion, claiming that it was the best for me. But they stuck to their religious principles, and are showing the world that people with AIDS are not to be feared; people with AIDS are to be loved.

Thus, a rare, blessed ministry of giving and receiving love, bravery displayed equally by congregants and clergy, persisted in the face of death.

Universalism beckons us to master the twin theologies of generosity and appreciation, giving and receiving. Some people say it is more blessed to give than to receive; others say, no, it is more blessed to receive than to give. What is truly blessed, says the Universalist way, is when we give, to give exuberantly and genuinely, and when we receive, to receive gratefully and joyously.

# Quintessential Bridger

*The Universalists may be wrong at a thousand points in their rendering of texts... but in the faith that the love of God for each particular soul will last as long as their justice and as long as eternity, they are not wrong.*
— *Thomas Starr King*

Thomas Starr King (1824-1864) practiced both wings of our merged faith—Universalism *and* Unitarianism. As Russell Miller recounts:

> It was King who, in his speech to Universalists in Faneuil Hall in 1858, contributed the often-quoted aphorism to the effect that Universalists believed that God was too good to damn them forever, while Unitarians believed that they were too good to be damned. King added, half jokingly, that the reason the two denominations had not united long ago was that they were really "too near of kin to be married."

Because King uncompromisingly straddled two traditions, he was often chastised; those who serve as bridges frequently get walked on by both sides.

In 1961, nearly one century after King died, these "twin-truths" of liberal Christianity did what King believed they should, namely, join together in creating a third reality, the Unitarian Universalist Association, which included yet transcended them both.

King bridged in other ways as well. He was a lover of nature, especially the New Hampshire mountains, about which he wrote in *The White Hills*, and the Yosemite landscape in California, one of whose peaks bears his name. Yet King was equally committed to the eradication of urban injustice, marked by his bicoastal, inner city ministries in Boston and San Francisco. Religious leaders have often been either naturalists or activists, but few have embodied a blend of both so effectively as did Thomas Starr King.

Small of stature, King cut a broad moral swath, exhibiting a huge heart and an expansive vision. What size he lacked in height, King made up for in boldness. When he arrived in San Francisco in 1860, King was greeted with questioning glances that seemed to ask: Could this slender young man with his beardless, boyish face, be the celebrated preacher, Thomas Starr King? King laughed in reply: "Though I weigh only 120 pounds, when I am mad, I weigh a ton." His righteous indignation was never more evident than when he helped keep the state of California from seceding from the Union during the agonizing days of the Civil War.

Thomas Starr King was a superior preacher, possessed of keen wit and intellect, whose theology demonstrated respect for both reason and faith. In 1844, he wrote to a friend saying, "reason was the very essence of faith, else faith is a blind idolatry. The true faith is the self-renunciation of reason where reason finds that it can know no farther." But as a practicing theologian, King was never swallowed up in metaphysical ether, keeping his feet planted firmly in the public realm. He served his era as an articulate philosopher and able politician, devoted to creating a spiritual republic for his age.

In our modern world so polarized by extremism, it is empowering to contain in our Universalist archives the story of so courageous a witness as Thomas Starr King, one who paid homage to both the yins and yangs of reality, a quintessential bridger.

# Universalism Lives On . . .

*Contributions from contemporary Universalists.*

⁓

My religious heritage traveled through four generations of women . . . four generations of Universalist women from rural western Ohio who passed along their Universalist faith to me through their daughters. Mary Disher Fudge was part of a large family who formed the Eldorado Church in 1849. Stern looking as pictures of her indicate, she surely possessed courage and a trust in God's love living on the frontier.

Her daughter, Jane Fudge Beard, demonstrated a generous, loving spirit, matched equally by her ample stature. How she felt the sting of inequality when she married and family land in her name was deeded to her husband by law. She was convinced that the love of God was equally distributed among men and women, although the law did not recognize it!

Grandmother Oma Beard Rautsaw was a loving, modest, steady woman. The pleasure of turning the soil for planting vegetables and flowers was equalled by her delight in tending all developing life and harvesting its luscious tastes and fragrant flowers.

Mother Dorothy Rautsaw Wynkoop is a lifelong example of living her Universalist faith. Diminished though her energy is now, in earlier years she brought her Universalist perspective to bear on school and community organizations. She was an institutionalist working for Universalist organizations in the local and national arenas, always speaking hopefully for youth and for the future of our Universalist faith.

My gratitude to these foremothers is beyond words.

—Nancy W. Doughty

I'm a Unitarian Universalist by choice, even though I'm a birthright participant. It is my choice, my free decision, to be a Unitarian Universalist. That shouldn't sound too strange, each of us starts with that freedom of decision.

Freedom is one of those flag-waving words. Often, to be free suggests no ties, no connections, no commitments—a free spirit. But that is freedom FROM. There is another freedom, our freedom TO: to decide, to dedicate, to covenant, to commit oneself.

Perhaps we have cherished the wrong freedom. I have a conviction that strength, support, loyalty, and commitment come from rallying around a commonly held belief, openly expressed and understood, accepted, and "owned" by each, that our community forms and comes to life around this concept.

Thus, my freedom is freedom TO: to join with others of like mind and spirit, to enlarge my circle of self, to expand my boundaries, to include. Free to commit myself to an institution, the church, the Unitarian Universalist Church.

—Phyllis B. McKeeman


Creedless though we are, we need not be spineless. As Universalists, we have at least three common denominators that offer the power to harmonize our fractional splinterings: fellowship, freedom, and a high estimate of human dignity brought about by education, the most noble character within our capacities. How much this world needs to recognize human dignity! Universalists living in a world spattered by the mud of insulting, scornful names need to be alerted to our basic humanity.

—Carl Westman

# The Love
# of God

# Everlasting Love of God

*This is the real nature of Universalism; it is a religion of ultimate and overwhelming confidence. It expresses the cosmic security of which we must be assured for joyous and creative living. God is loving; that love is sovereign.*
—Albert Ziegler

John Murray's homily doesn't close with "Give them, not Hell, but hope and courage. . . ." He gives his new, enthusiastic Universalist cohorts additional marching orders: "Do not push them deeper into their theological despair, but preach the kindness and everlasting love of God."

From the Universalist perspective, human hope and courage are ultimately grounded in and surrounded by the eternal embrace of the divine. The Universalist theological stool will wobble, eventually collapse, without all three legs in place: hope, courage, and God's love.

Refusing to believe in eternal punishment, Universalists were branded heretical, irresponsible, and subversive. At certain times, they were even shunned from societal tasks, denied positions on juries and the like, because they were deemed immoral. Yet their compassionate anthropology flowed directly from their merciful theology.

What does "the kindness and everlasting love of God" truly mean? It means that no matter how hard we humans work, we cannot create or earn our salvation, which remains the gracious gift of God. It means that no matter where we hide or how far we run, we cannot avoid God's inescapable presence. Even human free will, however obstinate, is no contest for the Universalist deity. It means that no matter how fractious the divisions and how extensive the destruction wreaked in human history, God's love will ultimately triumph.

Our human compassion, then, is in response to divine mercy. We can never repay the Creator, only respond. When we feel unconditionally loved by the Universe, then we are filled with hope and activated by courage. We pass God's love on, insistently yet imperfectly, to sisters and brothers, soil and sky, animals and plants, to all who hunger for healing and assurance.

Even criminals. If God isn't cruel to us, then we can't be spiteful toward others. Universalism helped rehabilitate the view of God from a vengeful being to a compassionate one. This radical view of God resulted in Universalist commitment to the abolition of capital punishment and sweeping penal reform. In 1791, Universalist Benjamin Rush wrote: "A belief in God's universal love to all his creatures, and that he will finally restore all those of them that are miserable to happiness, is a POLAR truth. . . . It establishes the equality of humankind—it abolishes the punishment of death for any crime—and converts jails into houses of repentance and reformation."

Divine retribution and human revenge were considered by Universalists to be depraved doctrines. Criminal justice reform was consistently the most unpopular cause undertaken by Universalists and required considerable courage. Their founder, John Murray, had himself been tossed into debtor's prison in London and regularly preached to prisoners in the New World.

We have come full circle. Universalism contends that all human beings are redeemable. There is always hope, for the most despicable and incorrigible among us, hope of being renewed on this earth and being saved for eternity.

So, hope, courage, and the love of God, these three have been equally important and mutually intertwining principles in the annals of Universalist history since its beginnings in 1793. With abiding gratitude for these virtues and their exemplars, we would pause to celebrate, then rise to serve, carrying the inspirational legacy of American Universalism forward into the ages.

# Universalism Lives On . . .

*Contributions from contemporary Universalists.*

―

The Unitarians were meeting in a nearby hotel, while we Universalists were convened in the downtown church. Both groups were involved in a momentous dialogue concerning the joint statement that would effect the merger of the two denominations. While we waited at one point for a reconsideration of the place of Jesus (the next day's newspaper headlines read: JESUS IN, JESUS OUT), someone brought forward a resolution reflecting not only recent efforts at extraterrestrial exploration, but the Universalist message of all-embracing love. It is a little-known resolution amidst all the attempts, before and since, to express our collective concerns about social issues; some even thought it facetious. Nonetheless it passed. And I think it still stands as a call to celebrate the fundamental love that encompasses the whole interdependent web of existence:

> Be it resolved that this 1959 biennial session of the Universalist Church of America . . . counsels the highest level of humane respect for such forms of life or societies as may be encountered in the universe.
> —Beverly A. Bumbaugh

―

"Preach," said John Murray, "the kindness and everlasting love of God." It was not long before Universalists expanded the phrase "God's love" to "God IS love," the motto of many a framed sampler hung in churches and homes across the continent. For our nineteenth-century spiritual forebears, those three short words encapsulated the heart of their Universalist faith; for some of us, they still do. For others, perhaps a change in their order is helpful. Gandhi, it will be remembered, first decided that God is Truth, later revising this to Truth is God. "Love is God" makes religious sense, too, with or without the sampler.

Preaching "the everlasting love of God" is a pretty overwhelming assignment for most of us these days, those three words—"everlasting," "love," and "God"—are hard enough to handle separately, much less together! But perhaps there's a clue in Murray's words to help us move from abstraction to concreteness. By preaching (and practicing) "kindness" we're at least making a good start on what Murray was urging people to do. Who knows? It may take us farther than we think!

—Charles A. Howe

Where the heart stirs,
    there moves Universalism.
The center holds us
    within its transformative power of love.
We know with a wholeness of spirit
    that God is love,
    that life is good,
    that people are created for goodness out of love,
    that in the final reckoning
        all shall be one.
When we hurt, when we are broken, when we become separated:
    Let us seek the center which holds.
    Let us remember the goodness for which we were
        created.

Let us be open to the transformative power of love
that moves within the heart of life,
and be whole once again.
—Elizabeth M. Strong

# Notes

### Introduction
"Go out into the highways. . . ." p. v: John Murray, quoted in Henry H. Cheetham, *Unitarianism and Universalism: An Illustrated History* (drawings by Roger Martin) (Boston: Beacon Press, 1962), p. 80.

"The heresy hunters. . . ." p. vi: Clinton Lee Scott, *These Live Tomorrow* (Boston: Beacon Press, 1964), p. 41.

"This argument is solid. . . ." p. vi: *Ibid.*, p. 35.

"Remember, there is One. . . ." p. vi: Alfred Cole and Clarence Skinner, *Hell's Ramparts Fell: The Life of John Murray* (Boston: The Universalist Publishing House, 1941), p. 170.

"At that early Massachusetts center. . . ." p. vii: Elmo A. Robinson, "The Universalist General Convention: From Nascence to Conjugation," *The Journal of the Universalist Historical Society*, 1969-1970, *VIII*:48.

### No-Hellites
"If one believes. . . ." p. 2: Angus MacLean, *The Wind in Both Ears* (Boston: Beacon Press, 1987), p. 81.

### Sailing the Straits
"False early conceptions. . . ." p. 4: Mary Ashton Rice Livermore, quoted in Clinton Lee Scott, *These Live Tomorrow* (Boston: Skinner House Books, 1987), p. 145.

### Let All Sorrows Ripen in Me
"We have become shabby. . . ." p. 7: Clarence Russell Skinner, quoted in "Clarence Skinner Speaks" (pamphlet) (Boston: Unitarian Universalist Association, 1986).

"There are some griefs. . . ." p. 8: May Sarton, "On Grief," in *Selected Poems of May Sarton*, eds. Serena Sue Hilsinger and Lois Byrnes, (New York: W. W. Nortorn, 1978), pp. 77-78.

"We cannot save. . . ." p. 8: May Sarton, "A Hard Death," *Ibid.*, p. 74.

### The Stuff of Eternity
"I have planted a hope. . . ." p. 10: Albert Q. Perry, "Rural Reflections," in *Church of the Larger Fellowship Bulletin* (Boston: Unitarian Universalist Association, 1986).

"Universalists are often asked. . . ." p. 10: Lewis B. Fisher, quoted in *Universalism in America*, ed. Ernest Cassara (Boston: Beacon Press, 1971), p. 253.

"A belief has arisen. . . ." p. 10: Benjamin Rush, quoted in Paul L'Herrou, *Unitarian Universalist Heritage, 1978-1979, A Collection of Readings* (Boston: Unitarian Universalist Association, Pacific Southwest District Grant).

"We have risen and not fallen;. . . ." p. 11: Marion D. Shutter, quoted in Russell Miller, *The Larger Hope*, Volume II (Boston: Unitarian Universalist Association, 1985), p. 105.

"The case for hope. . . ." p. 11: Norman Cousins, *Human Options* (New York: W.W. Norton, 1981), p. 57.

## The Larger Hope

"Religion which is compartmentalized. . . ." p. 13: Dorothy T. Spoerl (adapted), *What is Religious about Religious Education?* (pamphlet) (Boston: Unitarian Universalist Association), p. 2.

"Any Universalism worthy of. . . ." p. 13: Robert Cummins, quoted in Russell Miller, *The Larger Hope*, Volume II (Boston: Unitarian Universalist Association, 1985), p.643.

## Hopedale and Salubria

"My hope was too large. . . ." p. 15: Adin Ballou, quoted in Henry H. Cheetham, *Unitarian Universalism* (Boston: Beacon Press, 1962), p. 98.

"His theology was. . . ." p. 16: Clinton Lee Scott, *These Live Tomorrow* (Boston: Skinner House Books, 1987), p. 112.

"We must not only preach. . . ." p. 16: Cheetham, p.97.

"I believe that the whole universe. . . ." p. 16: Abner Kneeland, quoted in *Universalism in America*, ed. Ernest Cassara (Boston: Beacon Press, 1971), p. 167.

## Happiness and Holiness Are Inseparable

"And I took it so. . . ." p. 18: George de Benneville, quoted in *Universalism in America,* ed. Ernest Cassara (Boston: Beacon Press, 1971), p. 53.

When I am an old woman. . . ." p. 19: Betty Mills, adapted from Jenny Joseph, "Warning" in *When I Am An Old Woman I Shall Wear Purple,* ed. Sandra Martz (Watsonville, CA: Papier-Mache Press, 1987), p. 1.

## Grand Possibilities Are All Before Us

"From the moment I believed. . . ." p. 21: Augusta Jane Chapin, quoted in Susan Gitlin-Emmer, *Roots of Our Strength* (Unitarian Universalist Association, Pacific Southwest District Grant, 1980), p. 27.

"We need spiritual giants. . . ." p. 22: Clarence Skinner, "The World Tomorrow" (June 1940), quoted in Henry H. Cheetham, *Unitarianism and Universalism: An Illustrated History* (drawings by Roger Martin) (Boston: Beacon Press, 1962), p. 113.

"We are still in the dawn...." p. 22: Augusta Jane Chapin, quoted in *Not Hell, But Hope: The John Murray Distinguished Lectures (1987-1991)*, ed. Charles A. Howe (Lanoka Harbor, NJ: The Murray Grove Association, 1991), p. 66.

### Benevolence

"Conduct is three-fourths...." p. 28: P. T. Barnum, quoted in *Universalism in America*, ed. Ernest Cassara (Boston: Beacon Press, 1971), p. 244.

"By this Starbuck seemed to mean...." p. 29: Herman Melville, *Moby Dick* (New York: New American Library, 1961) p. 122.

"As the years passed...." p. 29: Elmo Robinson, *Journal of Liberal Ministry*, Vol. XI, No. 3 (Boston: Unitarian Universalist Association, 1971), p. 46.

"Parson, I used to think...." p. 30: Abraham Lincoln, quoted in John Nichols Booth, *Introducing Unitarian Universalism* (Boston: Unitarian Universalist Association, 1986), p. 10.

### Let Love Continue

"Let love continue...." p. 32: Hosea Ballou, quoted in Mark Morrison-Reed, *How Open the Door: Afro-Americans' Experience in the Unitarian Universalist Association* (Unitarian Universalist Association, 1989), p. 28.

"The ultimate measure...." p. 32: Martin Luther King, Jr., quoted in Coretta Scott King, *The Words of Martin Luther King, Jr.* (New York: New Market Press, 1983), p. 24.

### Agitators for Equality

"Each true life...." p. 35: Phebe A. Hanaford, *Daughters of America* (Augusta, ME: True and Company, 1882), p. 6.

"Yes,... our souls...." p. 35: Judith Sargent Murray, "On the Equality of the Sexes," quoted in Susan Gitlin-Emmer, *Roots of Our Strength* (Boston: Unitarian Universalist Association, Pacific Southwest District Grant, 1980), p. 78.

"In over ten years...." p. 36: Russell Miller, *The Larger Hope*, Volume I (Boston: Unitarian Universalist Association, 1979), p. 545.

"Her booking agents...." p. 37: Clinton Lee Scott, *These Live Tomorrow* (Boston: Beacon Press, 1964), pp. 143-144.

"I congratulate women...." p. 37: Miller, *The Larger Hope*, Volume I, p. 573.

### Patriots, One and All

"The wish to promote...." p. 39: Sarah Josepha Hale, quoted in Sherbrooke Rogers, *Sarah Josepha Hale: A New England Pioneer, 1788-1879* (Grantham, NH: Tompson and Rutter, 1985), p. 13.

"The sober truth. . . ." p. 40: Daniel Bragg Clayton, quoted in Russell Miller, *The Larger Hope*, Volume I (Boston: Unitarian Universalist Association, 1979), p. 508.

"Today's surgeons. . . ." p. 41: Stephen Fritchman, "UUSC Annual Meeting Address," June 24, 1976 (Boston: Unitarian Universalist Service Committee).

## Circuit Riders

"I have written everything. . . ." p. 42: Caroline Augusta White Soule, quoted in Susan Gitlin-Emmer, *Roots of Our Strength* (Boston: Unitarian Universalist Association, Pacific Southwest District Grant, 1980), p. 109.

"In the two years of 1904 and 1905. . . ." p. 43: Quillen Shinn, quoted in Russell Miller, *The Larger Hope*, Volume II (Boston: Unitarian Universalist Association, 1985), p. 352.

"I was always tired. . . ." p. 43: Caroline Soule, quoted in Catherine Hitchings, "Unitarian and Universalist Women Ministers," *Journal of the Universalist Historical Society*, 1975, X:136.

## Reluctant Reformers for Racial Justice

"We believe it to be inconsistent. . . ." p. 45: Benjamin Rush, quoted in Henry H. Cheetham, *Unitarianism and Universalism* (Boston: Beacon Press, 1962), p. 88.

"The Universalist idea of God. . . ." p. 45: Clarence R. Skinner, quoted in Ernest Cassara, *Universalism in America* (Boston: Beacon Press, 1971), p. 250.

"After all,. . . ." p. 46: Russell Miller, *The Larger Hope*, Volume I (Boston: Unitarian Universalist Association, 1979), p. 574. [The quote beginning "one of the distinguishing. . . ." is from *Universalist Miscellany*, February 1846, 3:319.]

"Every child must know. . . ." p. 47: Joseph Fletcher Jordan, quoted in Denise Tracy, *A Stream of Living Souls (Stories for Home and Worship), Volume II* (Oak Park, IL: Delphi Resources, 1987), p. 83.

"The racism that pervades. . . ." p. 47: Whitney Young, *Beyond Racism: Building an Open Society* (New York: McGraw-Hill Book Co., 1969), p. 255.

"America is racist. . . ." p. 47: William Jones, "Beyond Racism: The New Agenda for Religious Liberals," lecture series, February 8-11, 1988 (Madison, WI: Meadville/Lombard Winter Institute).

## Lovers Tossed by These Difficult Times

"Know that the love. . . ." p. 49: Mark Mosher DeWolfe, from his address to the Toronto AIDS Awareness Week candlelight vigil, June 1987 (unpublished).

"I am not fussy. . . ." p. 49: Greta Crosby, from "Spiritual Odyssey," an address given at Prairie Star Professional Religious Leaders' Conference, April 3, 1978 (unpublished).

"By sharing leadership. . . ." p. 50: Mark Mosher DeWolfe, "Love and Let Love," *Christianity and Crisis*, July 4, 1988: 222-223.

### Quintessential Bridger

"The Universalists may be wrong. . . ." p. 52: Thomas Starr King, quoted in Elmo Robinson, "The Universalist Connections of Thomas Starr King," *Annual Journal of the Universalist Historical Society*, 1964-1965, V:23.

"It was King who, . . ." p. 52: Russell Miller, *The Larger Hope*, Volume I (Boston: Unitarian Universalist Association, 1979), p. 831.

"Reason was the very essence. . . ." p. 53: Thomas Starr King, quoted in Miller, *Ibid.*, p. 830.

### Everlasting Love of God

"This is the real nature. . . ." p. 58: Albert Ziegler, *Foundations of Faith* (Boston: Universalist Publishing House, 1959), p. 20.

"A belief in God's universal love. . . ." p. 59: Benjamin Rush, quoted in George Hunston Williams, *American Universalism* (Boston: Skinner House Books, 1971), p. 59.

# Selected Resources

Cassara, Ernest, *Hosea Ballou: The Challenge to Orthodoxy* (Washington, D.C.: University Press of America, 1961, 1982).

Cassara, Ernest, editor, *Universalism in America: A Documentary History* (Boston: Beacon Press, 1971).

Cheetham, Henry, *Unitarianism and Universalism: An Illustrated History* (Drawings by Roger Martin) (Boston: Beacon Press, 1962).

Cole, Alfred S. and Clarence R. Skinner, *Hell's Ramparts Fell: The Life of John Murray* (Boston: The Universalist Publishing House, 1941).

Gitlin-Emmer, Susan, *Roots of Our Strength: A Heritage of Unitarian and Universalist Women* (Publication made possible by a grant from the Unitarian Universalist Association, Pacific Southwest District, 1980.)

Hitchings, Catherine F., "Universalist and Unitarian Women Ministers," *The Journal of the Universalist Historical Society*, Volume X, 1975 (Boston: Universalist Historical Society, 1975).

Howe, Charles A., editor, *Not Hell, But Hope: The John Murray Distinguished Lectures (1987-1991)* (Lanoka Harbor, NJ: The Murray Grove Association, 1991).

Howe, Charles A., *The Larger Faith: A Short History of Universalism* (Boston: Skinner House Books, 1993).

L'Herrou, Paul, *Unitarian Universalist Heritage, 1978-1979, A Collection of Readings* (Publication made possible by a grant from the Unitarian Universalist Association, Pacific Southwest District, 1976.)

MacLean, Angus H., *The Wind in Both Ears* (Boston: Unitarian Universalist Association, 1965, 1987).

MacPhee, John Stewart, compiler, *The Tao of Universalism: The Thoughts, Teachings and Writings of Dr. John Murray Atwood* (New York: Vantage Press, 1989).

McKeeman, Gordon B., editor, *To Meet the Asking Years* (Boston: Unitarian Universalist Association, 1983).

Miller, Russell, *The Larger Hope: The First Century of the Universalist Church in America, 1770-1870* (Boston: Unitarian Universalist Association, 1979).

Miller, Russell. *The Larger Hope: The Second Century of the Universalist Church in America, 1870-1970* (Boston: Unitarian Universalist Association, 1985).

Robinson, Elmo A., "Universalism, A Changing Faith," *The Journal of the Universalist Historical Society*, Volume II, 1960-1961 (Boston: Universalist Historical Society, 1961).

Robinson, Elmo A., "The Universalist General Convention: From Nascence to Conjugation," *The Journal of the Universalist Historical Society*, Volume VIII, 1969-1970 (Boston: Universalist Historical Society, 1970).

Scott, Clinton Lee, *Religion Can Make Sense* (Boston: Universalist Publishing House, 1949).

Scott, Clinton Lee, *These Live Tomorrow: Twenty Unitarian Universalist Biographies* (Boston: Beacon Press, 1964).

Scott, Clinton Lee, *The Universalist Church of America: A Short History* (Boston: Universalist Historical Society, 1957).

Tracy, Denise, *A Stream of Living Souls: Stories for Home and Worship, Volume II* (Oak Park, IL: Delphi Resources, 1987).

Williams, George Hunston, *American Universalism: A Bicentennial Historical Essay* (Boston: Skinner House Books, 1971).

Ziegler, Albert F., *Foundations of Faith: Conversations on a Theological Approach to Universalism* (Boston: Universalist Publishing House, 1959).

# Index of Universalist Contributors

Ballou, Adin ..................................................... 15
Ballou, Hosea .................................................. 32
Barnum, P.T. ................................................... 28
Bumbaugh, Beverly A. ..................................... 61
Chapin, Augusta Jane ...................................... 21
Cummins, Drusilla ........................................... 24
de Benneville, George ..................................... 18
DeWolfe, Barbara Mosher ............................... 24
DeWolfe, Mark Moser ..................................... 49
Doughty, Nancy W. .......................................... 54
Gaines, Charles ............................................... 25
Gooding, Margaret K. ...................................... 26
Hale, Sarah Josepha ........................................ 39
Hanaford, Phebe A. ......................................... 35
Howe, Charles A. ............................................. 61
King, Thomas Starr ......................................... 52
Livermore, Mary Ashton Rice ........................... 4
MacLean, Angus ............................................... 2
McKeeman, Phyllis B. ...................................... 55
Perry, Albert Q. ............................................... 10
Rush, Benjamin ............................................... 45
Skinner, Clarence Russell Skinner ................... 7
Soule, Caroline Augusta White ....................... 42
Spoerl, Dorothy ............................................... 13
Strong, Elizabeth M. ........................................ 62
Westman, Carl ................................................. 55
Ziegler, Albert ................................................. 58